BEST OF
COFFEE SHOP DESIGN

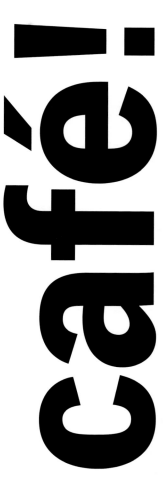

Imprint
The Deutsche Nationalbibliothek lists this publication in the Deutsche Nationalbibliografie;
detailed bibliographical data are available on the internet at http://dnb.d-nb.de.

ISBN 978-3-03768-045-2
© 2010 by Braun Publishing AG
www.braun-publishing.ch

2nd edition 2011

Project coordinator: Annika Schulz
Editorial staff: Jennifer Sandner, Rebecca Wrigley
Translation: Alice Bayandin
Graphic concept: Michaela Prinz

BEST OF
COFFEE SHOP DESIGN

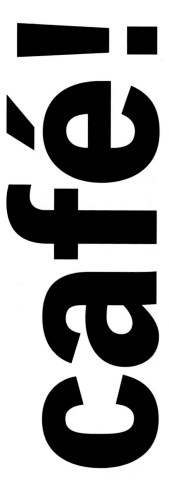

BRAUN

Preface

Dagmar Glück

Coffee is the international cult drink. Famous architects and aspiring interior designers the world over have made it their task to create spaces where the bean's aroma can properly unfold. "Café! Best of Coffee Shop Design" shows 43 unique café designs. From New York to Tokyo to Vienna, the current projects pay homage to the centuries-old coffeehouse tradition while setting new trends.

The coffeehouse was once a dignified place for coffee and cake. However, after the coffee shop revolution of the recent years, coffee isn't just coffee anymore – mocha, macchiato or mélange are now a must-have on the menu. It's not just the way we take our caffeine that is determined by our tastes, but the question of where is just as important, and the competition is fierce. Creative concepts that offer customers an additional aesthetic value and differentiate themselves from the big chains are in high demand; the designers' stylistic bandwidth is matched only by the length of the drinks menu. Some designs are minimalist and reduced, pure like a black shot of espresso. Others are playful, futurist or opulent like a caramel frappuccino with extra whipped cream.

Coffee itself can be a design's leitmotif. It is found in the color palette and form selection in the Juan Valdez Flagship Café in New York. Hariri & Hariri Architecture were inspired by the shape of the coffee bean; using modern materials, they combined Columbian connection to the earth with the pulse of the U.S. metropolis.

Columbia is a big coffee exporter, but coffee comes originally from the Ethiopian highlands in Africa. According to the legend, a shepherd by the name of Kaldi discovered coffee in the 9th century A.D. He noticed that his goats became much more animated after picking the berries off the bushes. Kaldi tried the fruits himself, and experienced the same invigorating effects. He showed his discovery to some monks, who spat the beans out into the fire because they were so bitter. They were amazed by the pleasant aroma that the beans developed when roasted. The first cup of coffee was on its way, and the drink quickly spread across the Ottoman Empire, with cafés appearing in Cairo, Damascus and Aleppo.

Europeans had to wait to get their fix until 1647, when the first Italian café opened in Venice. Italians invented numerous coffee specialties and established the cornerstone of today's coffee culture. In Austria, the Viennese coffeehouse is a true institution. Here, the guest has all the time in the world to read the newspaper accompanied by a single cup of coffee, without feeling forced to give up his place for a new customer.

Cafés are places of communication, a fact which certainly has its causes in caffeine's invigorating effects. This is where revolutions have been planned, novels written, and where oddballs and players cross their paths. For this reason, more so than other spaces, the café challenges its architects in a multitude of ways. The designer has to create a communicative and inspirational place which can simultaneously answer to all practical requirements of a functional catering business. Accordingly, the used materials have to be robust and easy-to-clean. Panoramic windows should provide an inviting glimpse of the interior to passers-by, while affording a pleasant view to guests inside. Because per-customer sales in cafés are comparatively low, most space concepts ensure maximum flexible seat occupancy which can still provide waiter access and avoids crowding the guest. To properly present the goods and guarantee seamless self-service, if needed, the overall concept is often dominated by a central bar.

In the TATE Café in Malta, the Matthew James Mercieca Design Architects team went as far as to transform the bar into a sculpture. The brushed aluminum eye-catcher stretches up to the vaulting tunnel-like limestone ceiling, creating a captivating juxtaposition between archaic and modern. Innovative lighting technology helps transform the TATE into a happening bar when the dark sets in. Such metamorphoses are included in many design concepts, making conversions from café to lounge or restaurant effortless.

It is often required to integrate a café into a overarching spatial concept, for example as part of a showroom or shop. A successful example of this is the Barbie Café on the top floor of the flagship Barbie Store in Shanghai. Slade Architecture has embraced the cult doll and infused its charm into every minute detail, creating a princess dream in black, white and pink. Motto Café in Vienna also features dolls, albeit of a less feminine kind. The design by BEHF is eerie but beautiful, using doll torsos as ceiling stucco and doll heads as candle holders. Lavender-colored upholstered furniture is quilted and covered with a transparent plastic foil which plays with reflections of evening lights. The hip Motto Café is an ironic reminiscence of the Viennese coffeehouse tradition.

Less private than your personal living room, the café is a homey retreat for the first date, a chat with your best friend or a casual business meeting. As a half-public space, the café is an oasis in the city not just due to its hot drink – when its design is as appealing and imaginative as the projects presented here, it easily becomes a paradise for all caffeine addicts and passionate milk foam sippers.

Afro Cafe | Salzburg | AFRO COFFEE

The colors and designs are a celebration of contemporary African culture

Aroma Espresso Bar 72nd Street | New York | Studio Gaia

This design uses vibrant colors, playful wall graphics and designer chairs made for lingering

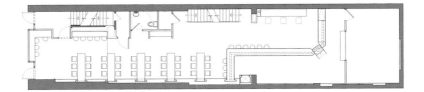

The architects chose a **simple** and **striking palette:** black lacquer, white accents, **pink upholstery** and curtains

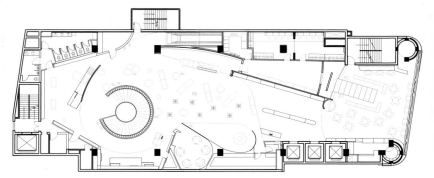

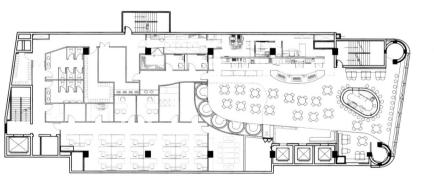

Yo

Organically shaped
tables and chairs blend
into the white backdrop

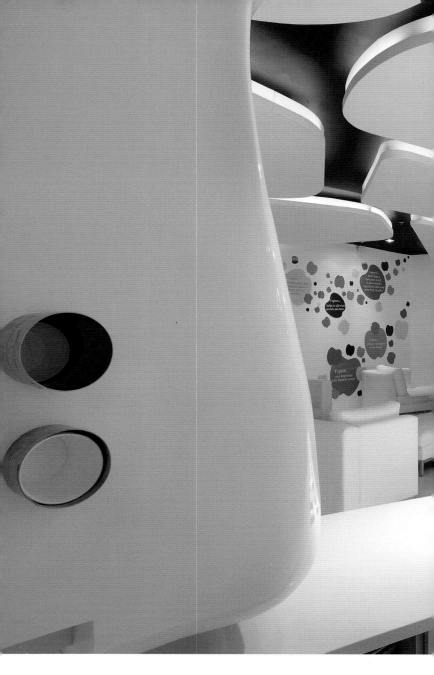

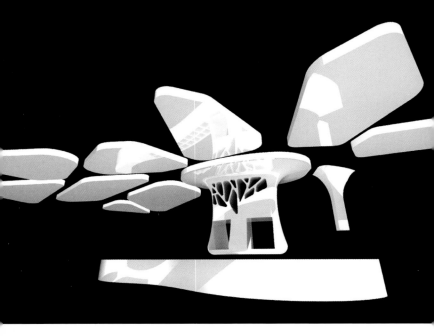

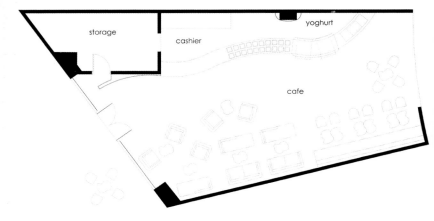

storage

cashier

yoghurt

cafe

A **moving bench** allows to sit underneath a semicircular **fluorescent lamp.**

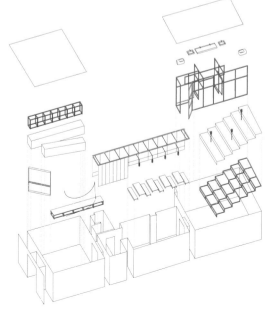

A dynamic and contemporary cultural site

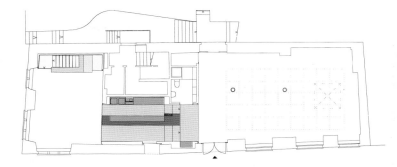

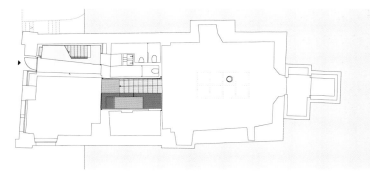

Every **possible material**
was employed for the design of
this extravagant café

NUDIMO:

TOAST 7,00
SIR 12,00
MASLINE 10,00

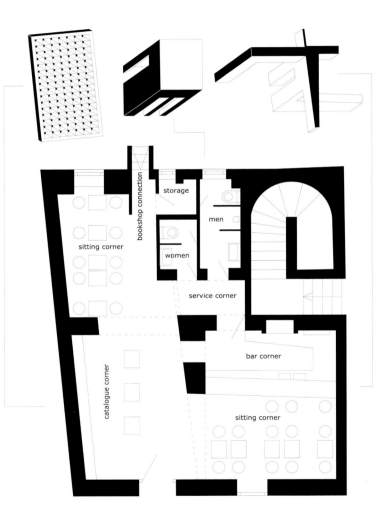

bookshop connection

storage

men

women

sitting corner

service corner

catalogue corner

bar corner

sitting corner

| **Café in Sintra** | Sintra | EXTRASTUDIO arquitectura, urbanismo e design lda

With the **existing rear-windows** and a **new vaulted space,** a **seamless transition** between walls and ceiling **is created**

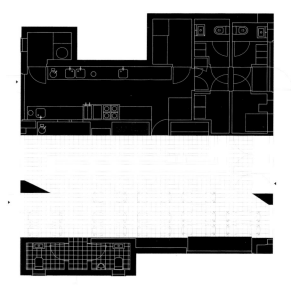

Café in the Park & Lobby Lounge | Osaka | GWENAEL NICOLAS, CURIOSITY

CAFÉ IN THE PARK
seasonal buffet

A welcoming bright modern lounge: dramatic and attractive

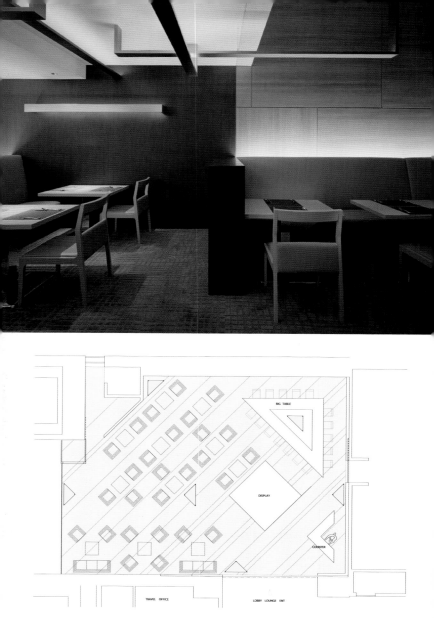

BIG TABLE

DISPLAY

COUNTER

TRAVEL OFFICE

LOBBY LOUNGE ENT

TOTAL   50 席

Café la Miell | Niihama City | suppose design office / Makoto Tanijiri

The **appeal of this café** lies in the **coherence in material** and color

Forever retro

Café Mochamojo I Bandra I Planet 3 Studios

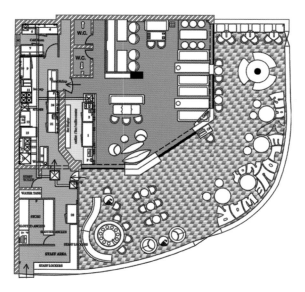

Tasteful, straightforward, gorgeous

TRINKEN

Willkommen im Cafe Rekord: zu den grünsten
Tees, den minzigsten Mojitos, den malzigsten
Bierchen von Flingern

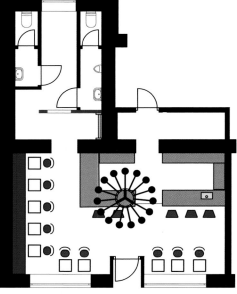

With its **pleasant** atmosphere, **the café** is **an oasis** for a **moment of relaxation**

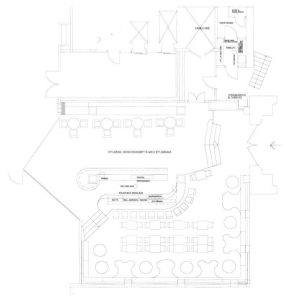

KYLBÄNK, BEREONINGSYTA MED KYLRÄNNA

VARUHISS

TORKFÖRRÅD

DISKMASKIN
& DISKHO

KASSA   DRICKA
                DRYCKESKYL

GOLVBRUNN

KYLAR MED DRAGLÅDA
                SBASKÅP/CADA

KAFFE   BÄLLANHANDEL MICRO   KYLVÄRRA

The space **is divided** into bar and shop **by a glass wall,** creating a seamless transition

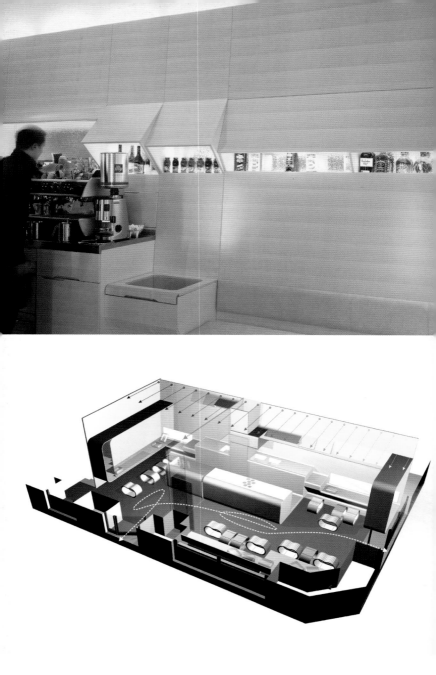

A stylish and urbane café the design is characterized by the color palate

The walls **are stucco** and painted in the **color "café latte"**

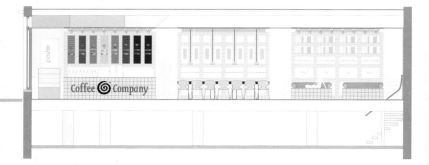

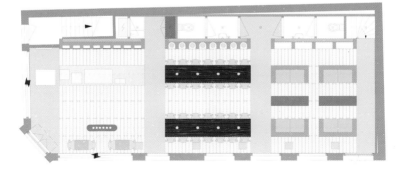

A great amount **of openness** was required because the **shop** is **prominently** situated in an **atrium**

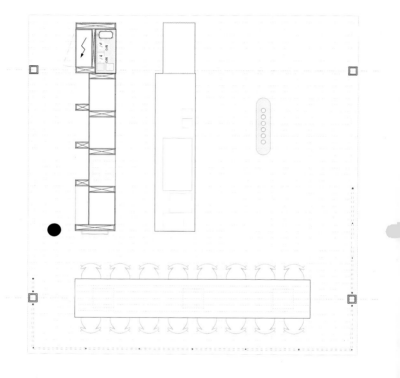

Contemporary café design meets Victorian ballroom

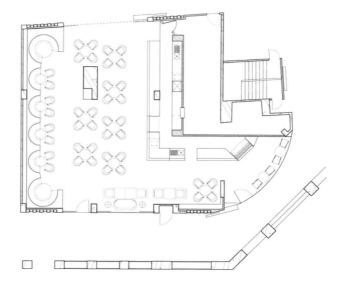

tcc

the coffee connoisseur

The **concrete elements** serve as both **structure** and **furniture**

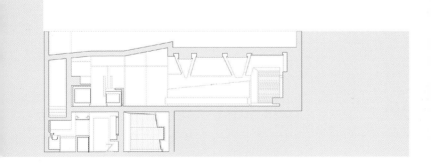

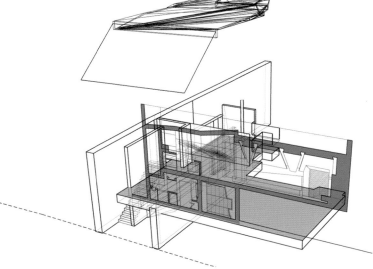

Radiant colors
and flowing lines create a
dynamic atmosphere

Involving **all senses** through **music,** artistic images, **soft lighting** and **delicious tastes** and aromas

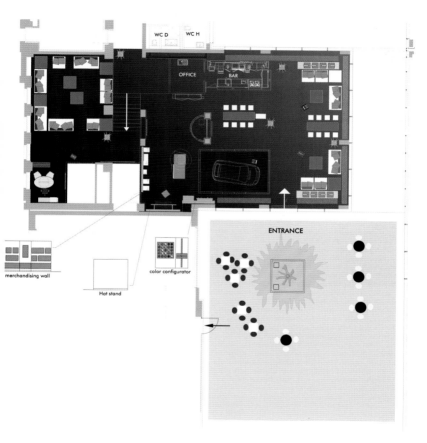

WC D

WC H

OFFICE

BAR

ENTRANCE

merchandising wall

Hat stand

color configurator

Flowing shapes from Asian architecture interact with elements of modernity and its proportions

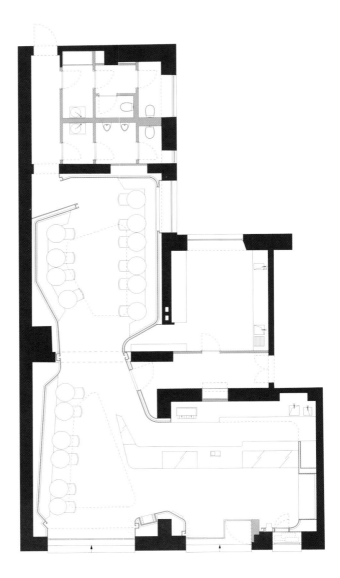

The **counters** and the **space itself** are transformed into **coffee chutes**

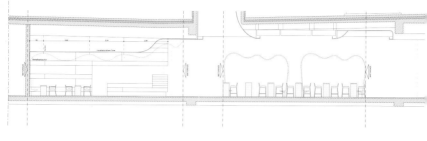

| **HOLLYS COFFEE brand identity** | Daejeon | BEYOND THE VOID

ntemporary
Romanticism

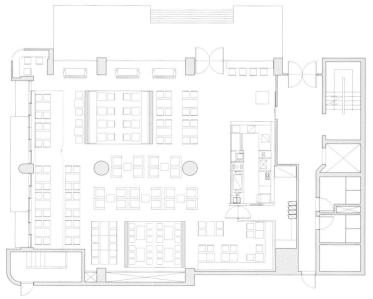

Hopkins Café | Baltimore | Kroiz Architecture with Ziger/Snead

The café refines **familiar laboratory** surfaces, **stainless equipment** and light **boxes**

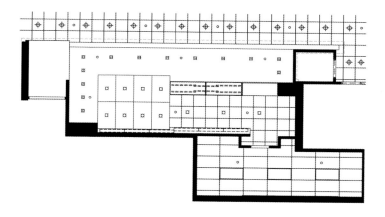

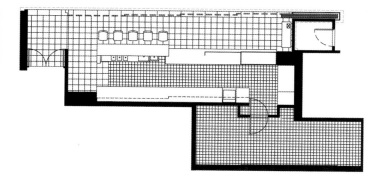

A **mixture** of **modern and** historic

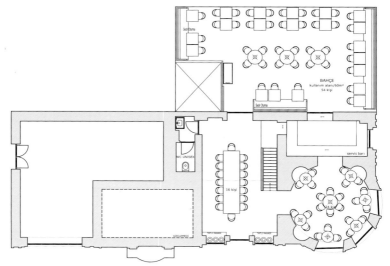

Made of glass, steel and **walnut** wood

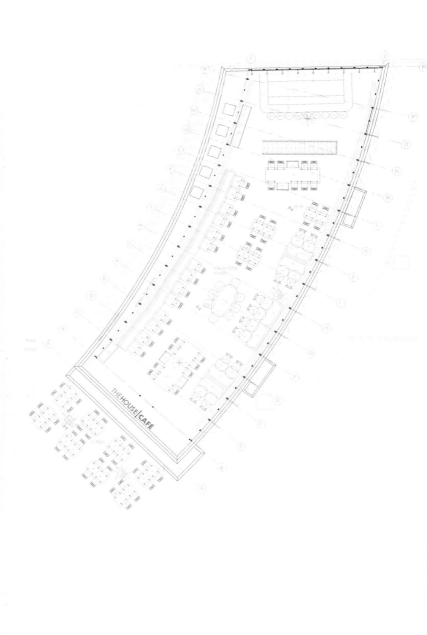

The **variety** of architectural materials **reflects different** characteristics of **coffee:** exclusive, **warm,** earthbound and **eclectic**

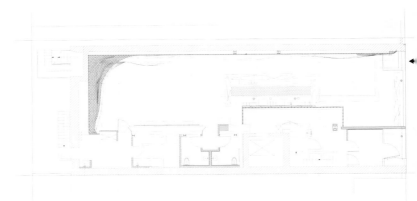

The designer's aim was to offer a fairytale feeling for children as well as an adult atmosphere for their parents

STORE

STORE

LOCKER

TOILET

STORE

PLAY ROOM

LIBRARY

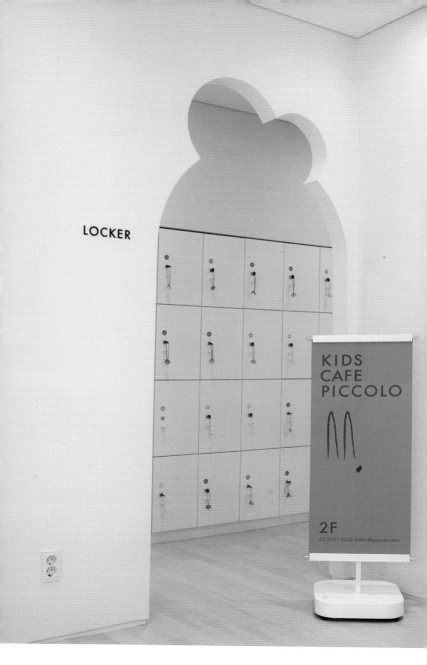

LOCKER

KIDS
CAFE
PICCOLO

2F
02-2201-3252 kidscafepiccolo.com

The **display fixture** is formed with a **frame of** **steel** and green beer **bottles**, and looks **like a tree**

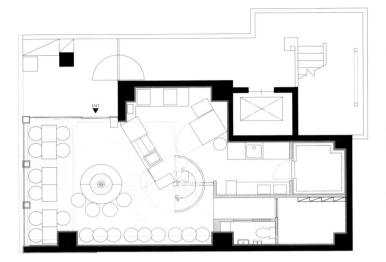

Tasse Kaffee	€			
Becher Kaffee	1,60			
Café Crème	2,10	Espresso macchiato	€	
Café mit Aroma	1,70	Espresso con panna	1,85	Milchkaffee, klein	€
Caffè ristretto	1,95	Cappuccino Classico	1,85	Café au lait	1,95
Espresso	1,90	Cappuccino Cremissimo	2,20	Latte	
Espresso lungo	1,70	Cappuccino con caramel	2,55	Latte macchiato	
Espresso doppio	1,70	Nutella Cappuccino	2,55	Latte macchiato doppio	3,00
	2,60	Cappuccino doppio	2,60	Nutella Latte Macchiato	3,25
		Milchkaffee, groß	3,10	Café Orhoffee, groß	2,90
			2,50	Tasse Kakao	3,10

Authentic materials that display **their composition** on open surfaces are the **basic elements** of the design concept

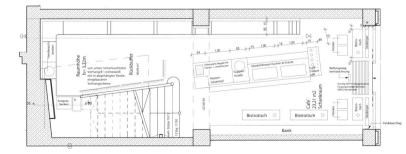

The contrast between contemporary design and antique elements defines this truly elegant café

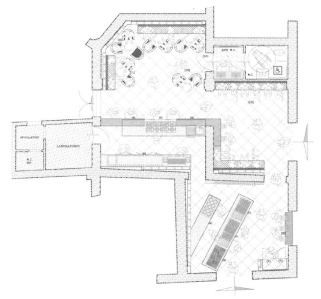

Steel **sculptures,** fire wood **slats** and playful **green walls** create an **artistic,** handcrafted **interior**

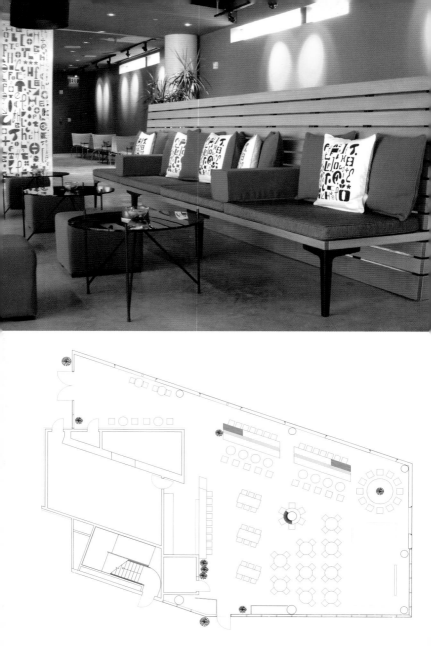

The architectural **perception** is based on many facets: **sensitive shades** of colors, **ingenious details** and superior materials

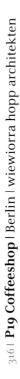

Red, green and simple –
the P19 Coffeeshop has no need
for gimmickry

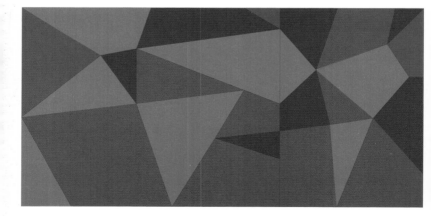

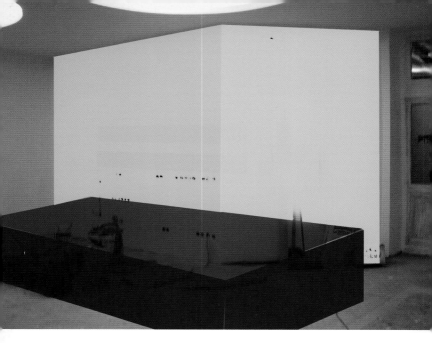

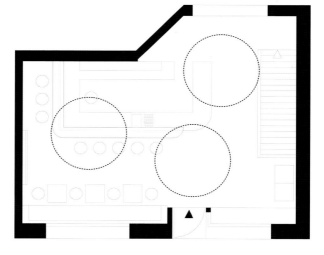

Spoon Café | Tokyo | emmanuelle moureaux architecture + design

Natural materials, light colors and overall brightness generate a cozy and warm atmosphere

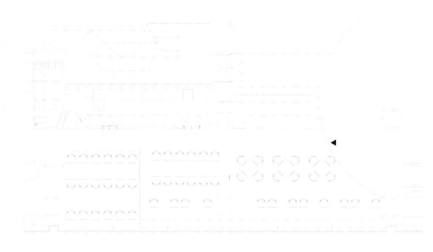

The **large screen** transforms this **futuristic bar** into an **exclusive** cinema

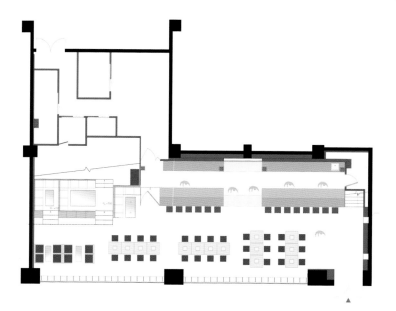

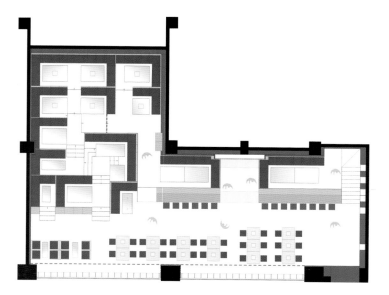

The 15th-century-**barrel vault** offers the perfect location for **an unusual** and **exciting** space

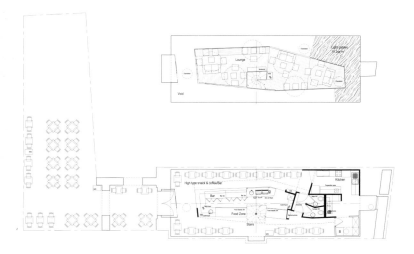

One of the **main objective** was **to create** a wide range different **seating experier** to suit **diverse purposes** and prefe

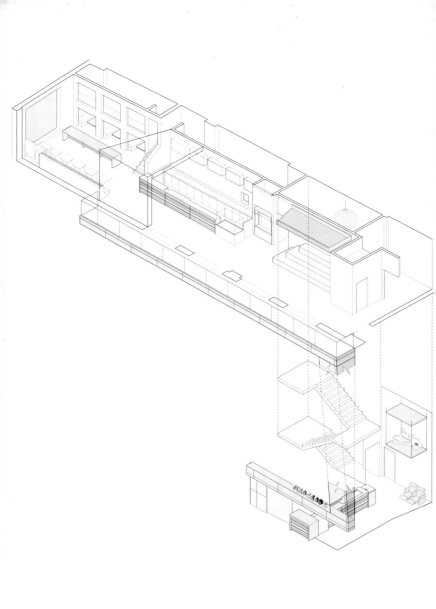

TIN

TINDERBOX-TO GO	S	R	L
LATTE		2.00	2.40
CAPPUCCINO	1.60	2.00	2.40
AMERICANO	1.35	1.80	2.25
FAIRTRADE FILTER	1.30	1.70	2.10
ESPRESSO		1.30	1.70
MACCHIATO		1.30	1.70
EXTRA SHOT/SYRUP/CREAM			0.40
SKINNY, SOYA, DECAF			FREE

AND SOME MORE...	R	L
HOT CHOCOLATE ORIGINAL, WHITE, SPICY	2.00	2.40
MOCHA ORIGINAL, WHITE, SPICY	2.40	2.80
CHAI LATTE	2.00	2.40
TEA: VARIOUS VARIETIES	FROM 1.70	
SOFT DRINKS		
SANDWICHES		
PASTRIES & CAKES		

Blue furniture and **unusual** shapes – the design of this **unique café** seems **extra-terrestrial**

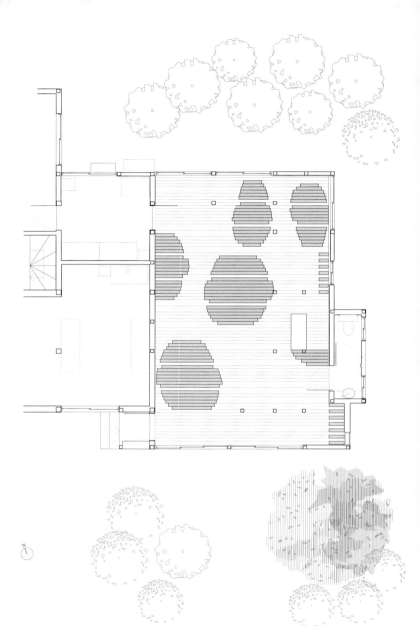

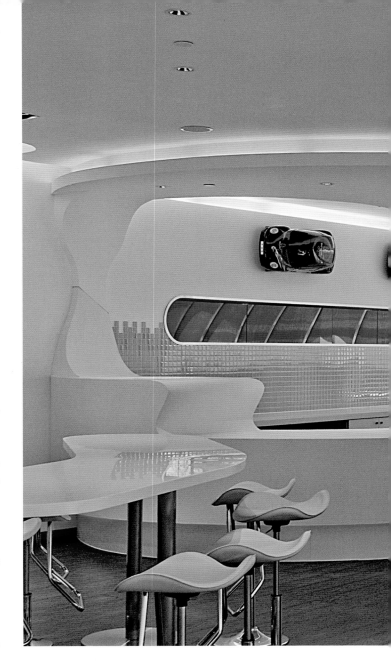

This **stylish café** offers a communication **platform** for **employees** and visitors

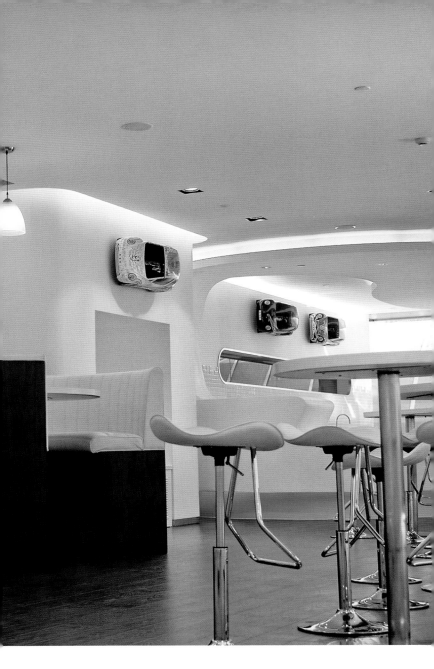

...castles in the air, your work need not be lost;
...where they should be. Now put the foundations under them.

HENRY DAVID THO...

The WALDEN was **created**
according to the
maxime of simplicity

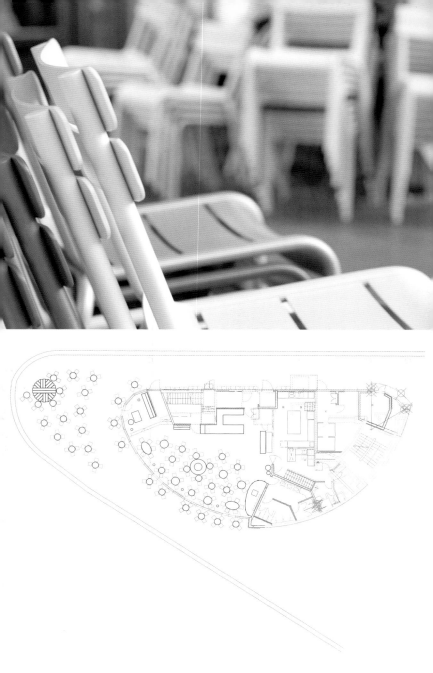

The **wall** is a **huge tiled surface** in a traditional **Indian pattern** that has been **abstracted** in shades of red and **orange**

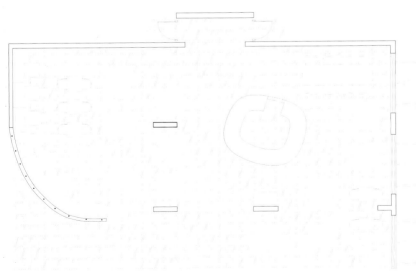

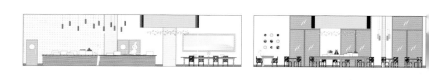

Architects Index

Picture Credits